Sir Wilfrid Laurier

#7

The weakling who stood his ground

Written by Heather Grace Stewart
Illustrated by Anna Payne-Krzyzanowski

Photo Credits
JackFruit Press would like to thank the Canadian
National Archives for photographs appearing on
pages 35 (PA-122657) and 41 (PA-135125).

© 2006 JackFruit Press Ltd.
Publisher—Jacqueline Brown
Editor—Helen Waumsley
Designer and Art Director—Marcel Lafleur
Researchers—Barbara Baillargeon, Peter Konieczny
and Hagit Hadaya

JackFruit Press Ltd.
Toronto, Canada
www.jackfruitpress.com

Library and Archives Canada Cataloguing in
Publication

Stewart, Heather Grace, 1972-   .

Sir Wilfrid Laurier: The weakling who stood his ground
/ Heather Grace Stewart; illustrator, Anna Payne-
Krzyzanowski.

(Canadian prime ministers: warts and all)

Includes index.

ISBN 0-9736406-3-4

1. Laurier, Wilfrid, Sir, 1841-1919—Juvenile literature.
2. Prime ministers—Canada—Biography—Juvenile
literature. 3. Canada—Politics and government—
1896-1911—Juvenile literature.
I. Payne-Krzyzanowski, Anna, 1955-   .
II. Title. III. Series.

FC551.L3S728 2005   j971.05'6'092
C2005-907335-7

Printed and Bound in Canada

...So, I'm here to show you around this really cool series of books on great Canadians.

This book tells the story of Sir Wilfrid Laurier, Canada's first French-speaking prime minister.

He was sick throughout most of his life but still managed to be a strong and inspiring leader!

Contents

Hot topics

Sir Wilfrid Laurier: A face

4

You see his face every time you reach for a $5 bill. Canada's seventh prime minister (and our first French-speaking one) was thin and weak and so frequently sick that he often thought he was dying. But he never let that stop him from becoming a great leader.

we see every day

Chances are, you see his face every week—without even realizing it. It happens every time you reach for a $5 bill. There he is, staring right back at you…Sir Wilfrid Laurier. Our seventh prime minister, Canada's first French-speaking leader, and the only one to serve our country for an unbroken 15 years. For these reasons (and many others we will look at in this book) Sir Wilfrid was immortalized on the Canadian $5 bill in 1969.

Born of humble folks

Canada's previous six prime ministers were either born in the British Isles or were the children of British-born parents. Wilfrid Laurier was our first prime minister whose ancestors had lived in **Lower Canada** (which we now call Quebec). And although Wilfrid is now known as "Sir Wilfrid Laurier," it is not a title he inherited. He was made a **Knight of the British Empire** (called a "Sir") after he became our prime minister. Wilfrid looked and dressed like our idea of an aristocrat, but his parents were humble folks who were not rich and had no connections to nobility or the rich merchants of Canada.

Wilfrid's father had to work long and hard to provide for his large family. In spite of all his hard work, three generations of Lauriers lived crammed together in a little wooden house in a small village. Life in the Laurier house was simple and everyone in the family helped out. Wilfrid's brothers hauled the family's drinking water from their well. His sisters spun the cloth the family wore. And all the kids got involved in making the candles that lit their home.

So who was this guy on our $5 bill? He was a Canadian proud of his French roots. His strong, rebellious spirit compelled him to defend the interests of anyone who was in need of justice. He was also a sensitive, almost shy man with a sweet soul and an amazing gift for speaking in

Want to know more? The words in bold are explained in the glossary at the back of the book.

public. Because of this great gift, Wilfrid was able to convince people of the rightness of his ideas. As we will see, Wilfrid was also an unusual man for his time because he was educated in both French and English. While born and raised a Roman Catholic, he had the opportunity to read the English Bible and live with two English-speaking families, one of whom was Protestant. This allowed him to understand Canada's two founding cultures in a way that few others could at the time.

Not bad for a "weakling"

Like many of our prime ministers, Wilfrid had some important personal obstacles to overcome. He was thin and weak—crummy at sports—and so frequently sick with a bad cough that he often thought he was dying. Do you think he craved the power that comes from being the prime minister? Nope. His friends actually had to convince him to run as a **member of Parliament**. And even then he wasn't sure he wanted to be prime minister. He often wondered if he was good enough to do the job. Yet Sir Wilfrid stayed in politics for all of 36 years.

As Canada's prime minister, he transformed our country in ways that few other leaders had done before or have done since. During his years in the prime minister's seat, Sir Wilfrid helped attract tens of thousands of immigrants to our west, created the provinces of Alberta and Saskatchewan, and established the Yukon as a territory. He created a new transcontinental railway and began building the Canadian navy.

Sir Wilfrid helped settle many important arguments between the English and the French. He helped Canada loosen its ties with Britain and achieve national unity. He fought the control that Roman Catholic bishops and priests held over the political lives of their parishioners. No matter what obstacle was flung in his way, Sir Wilfrid stepped over it and stood his ground. His vision for Canada lives on almost a century after his death.

This is because Sir Wilfrid had a clear picture of Canada. He dreamed of a unified and tolerant country where people of all racial and cultural backgrounds could live together in peace and harmony. His unique style of negotiation, based on compromise and conciliation (which means "becoming someone's friend"), set the pattern by which Canadians would be known in the times ahead. In that way, he showed us the best of what we could become as Canadians. During his life he was loved and admired by most, even his political opponents. Not bad for a sickly guy who seemed as if he were about to drop dead at any moment!

Some weakling! No matter what obstacle appeared in his way, Sir Wilfrid stepped right past it, probably coughing all the way!

Because of his amazing gift for speaking in public, Wilfrid becomes an inspiring politician who is able to convince people of the rightness of his ideas.

"My patriotism will consist in telling my country the hard truths which will waken it from its lethargy and make it enter into the true way of progress and prosperity."

Wilfrid makes this statement in his first address to the Quebec Assembly. Although he's really just starting out in politics, he's already spelled out the vision he will pursue his whole life.

1848

St-Lin is a quiet little Quebec village with two streets, several wooden houses, a mill pond, and a big grey stone church that dominates the countryside around it.

A proud descendent of French Canada's early settlers, Wilfrid's father is known for having his own opinions and not being afraid to argue with the parish priest.

An unusual boyhood

Wilfrid Laurier was born on November 20, 1841, in the village of St-Lin. St-Lin was a quiet little Quebec village with two streets, several wooden houses, a mill pond, and a big grey stone church that dominated the village and the countryside around it. You could see its steeple for miles and miles. St-Lin's folk talked to each other politely, and nothing much happened—unless you counted local gossip about **Carolus Laurier** (Wilfrid's father) and his latest argument with the Church. A proud, eighth-generation descendent of French Canada's early settlers, Carolus was known for having his own opinions and not being afraid of arguing his point with the parish priest.

Wilfrid? What kind of name is that?

Wilfrid's parents, **Marcelle Martineau** and Carolus Laurier, named him Henri Charles Wilfrid Laurier, but that's one heck of a mouthful, so they just called him Wilfrid. Besides being an easygoing, happy farmer, Wilfrid's father was also a land surveyor and lumber merchant. He was a loving and reasonable man who had a deep respect for spiritual values but believed that people should be allowed the freedom to think for themselves.

1841
Wilfrid is born in the tiny village of St-Lin, Canada East.

1841
Upper and Lower Canada are united. They become Canada West and Canada East.

1844
Wilfrid's sister, Malvina, is born.

1847
The St. Lawrence Canal is completed.

1848
Wilfrid's mother dies of tuberculosis.

1849
Wilfrid's father remarries. His new mom is Adéline, the woman who used to help his mother.

1852
Wilfrid is sent to live in New Glasgow.

9

Wilfrid's mother was sensitive, artistic, and read a lot. She was the one responsible for choosing Wilfrid's name. (The name "Wilfrid" was not an average French boy's name. It still isn't.) She had chosen that name from a Sir Walter Scott novel, *Ivanhoe*, a book about knights in armour who vowed to act with courage and honour. In the book, Wilfrid of Ivanhoe served his hero, Richard the Lionheart. Richard wanted to be King of the English and rid England of its French conquerors.

Wilfrid loved spending time with his mother, and probably inherited his gentle poetic nature from her. Because there was no formal schooling for boys in St-Lin until they turned 13, she taught Wilfrid to read and write. She painted pictures for him, read him stories, and told him about his heritage. While Wilfrid's father made him proud to be French Canadian, his mother gave him his love of French language and culture.

Three years after Wilfrid's birth, his sister **Malvina** was born and the Laurier family seemed destined to be quite happy. Unfortunately, this happiness was shattered by an illness that struck Wilfrid's mother when he was still only seven years old. She died of tuberculosis. Fortunately, **Adéline Éthier**, a woman who had been hired to help, was there to comfort Wilfrid and Malvina. Carolus married Adéline and she became Wilfrid's stepmother. Adéline was a warm, loving woman who would greet him with outstretched arms and hug him tenderly. Wilfrid soon had four half-brothers and sisters from his father's marriage to Adéline. His grandparents (Carolus's parents) also lived with them. The tiny Laurier house was so crowded that Wilfrid had to sleep on a thin shelf in a closet! Because of his fragile health, Wilfrid rarely worked outside in the fields, but could go with Carolus into the back roads as he did his surveying.

Then, when Malvina was just 11, she too died of the same disease that took their mother's life. Such deaths were common before effective treatment for tuberculosis was perfected during the 1950s and 60s.

Les Patriotes

Although St-Lin itself was quiet and peaceful, young Wilfrid actually lived during a turbulent time in Canada's history. Born only four years after the **Rebellion of 1837**, he had grown up listening to real stories about **Louis-Joseph Papineau**, a feisty French-Canadian nationalist leader. Papineau and his group of rebels (**Les Patriotes**) had tried to overthrow British rule in Lower Canada in a series of small battles. Wilfrid was deeply upset when he heard how Les Patriotes were defeated by the English army, many of the men executed, and Papineau forced to leave his homeland. Stories of this rebellion shaped Wilfrid as a young boy. His liberal-minded father told him that the Papineau-led rebels believed that they stood for justice and greater freedom. Obviously, patriotism alone wasn't enough.

Why was the Catholic Church so important in French Canada?

Nobody likes to lose. Not a hockey game, a basketball match, a chess game, or even a spelling bee. Can you imagine then how it feels to lose a real-life battle or a war? Imagine how it feels when your loved ones are killed, your home is wrecked, your town is destroyed, and your land is taken over by the very strangers you had been fighting.

That is how Canadiens (that's what French Canadians called themselves) felt after a battle on the **Plains of Abraham** back in 1759. Back then, they referred to this battle as "The Conquest." And many still do now, almost 250 years later. It was during this battle that a British army defeated the French forces in a colony called New France. This victory (or defeat, depending on which side you were on) was a turning point. Shortly after this battle, France handed over the colony to England. Then the French elite (the rich and educated people) returned to France, leaving the common folk to fend for themselves.

Most were in shock. They wondered what would happen to them. Would they be treated like their French neighbours, the **Acadians**? Only four years before (in 1755), 7,000 French colonists living in Acadia (what is now Nova Scotia) had been rounded up by the British army and forcibly shipped off to American **colonies** hundreds of miles away. Hundreds died on the way to their destinations. To make matters worse, the Canadiens were Catholics, whereas their new masters were mostly Protestants. Nowadays, that doesn't matter much because people have become more tolerant of each other. But back in 1759, it meant big trouble because the Catholics and Protestants (in France and in England) had been fighting (and killing) each other for centuries.

As the only French-speaking authority remaining in the former colony, the Catholic Church did what it could to avoid bloodshed and maintain law and order: it co-operated with the new British authorities. This greatly expanded the power and influence of the Church. Not only was it the dispenser of religious dogma (rules) and rituals, it was now the only source of French knowledge and culture.

What's more, the Church was now the go-between for the English authorities and the common folk. This meant that attending a Catholic school was now the only way to get the kind of education you needed. It also meant that "toeing the line" was the only way of making the kind of contacts you needed if you wanted to earn a living at anything other than farming or trapping.

A monstrance is a receptacle used to display a "consecrated host." Like all Catholics, young Laurier was taught that the wafer in that display case was the "body of Christ."

For more information about the Catholic Church, visit our website at www.jackfruitpress.com.

Wilfrid quickly became convinced that the best way to a peaceful Canada was compromise and understanding: the French and English would need to work together and learn about each other before any kind of national unity could be realized.

Since Canada was becoming increasingly British, Wilfrid's father thought his son's chances for success would increase if he grew up learning about the French and English cultures!

This gave Wilfrid a unique opportunity to grow up understanding both French and English much better than just about anyone else at the time.

Going to an English school! With the Scots?

It was Carolus who decided that his son should learn the ways of the English. So, when Wilfrid was not quite 11 years old, off he went to live with another family in New Glasgow, a village 10 kilometres away. Since that village was named after a famous town in Scotland, you can easily guess where many of its inhabitants had come from. Most of them were descendants of the Scottish soldiers who had occupied Quebec after the defeat of the French forces in 1759.

Wilfrid lived in New Glasgow for two years, quickly learning English and absorbing all that he could about the Protestant faith. This is how he developed tolerance for differences among people (this was way radical for that time—more than 100 years would pass before schools began teaching the importance of tolerance). He also learned a great deal about human relationships. Later, he recalled how he'd "fought with the Scotch boys, and made schoolboy love to the Scotch girls." But he admitted that he had much more success romancing the girls than winning fights with the boys. He learned that he'd rather solve a problem by using his head and his heart than fight it out with his fists!

A life-long passion for the English language

Wilfrid's love of reading and his love of the English language can be traced to the time he spent in New Glasgow. He went to school in a small wooden schoolhouse with only one window on each side. Wilfrid loved hearing his teacher read the classics. In the beginning, Wilfrid often didn't understand a single word because it wasn't just read in English—it was read in English by a teacher with a thick Scottish accent! But Wilfrid didn't mind; the words sounded beautiful to him.

When he wasn't going to school, Wilfrid lived with the Murrays, an English Protestant family. He also helped John Murray, the village tailor, serve English customers at the counter in his shop. Mr. Murray would often read to Wilfrid from the **King James Bible**. When Maman Adéline heard about this, she was not happy. The priests had taught her that mixing with non-Catholics was dangerous to one's soul! Wilfrid disagreed and wanted to stay with the Murrays, but his mother put her foot down. Because of this, Wilfrid had to live with the Kirkes, who also spoke English but were Irish Catholics. But soon it wouldn't matter. Soon he'd be living where much more would be expected of him—this time in French.

Wilfrid learns a lot by simply living with two English-speaking families in New Glasgow. This is also where he develops a love of reading and a passion for the English language.

When he isn't in school, Wilfrid helps John Murray serve customers in his tailor shop. A Protestant, Mr. Murray often reads to Wilfrid from the King James Bible. This is a novel experience for Wilfrid, because Catholics are not encouraged to read the Bible.

The Collège de l'Assomption's mission is to prepare boys to become priests. Instead of sitting at desks, students write on long wooden doors placed atop sawhorses. Classes are heated with wood-burning stoves and lit with oil lamps.

School discipline is strict and demanding. When Wilfrid is caught skipping classes (to watch legal proceedings at a nearby courthouse), he is forced to kneel for an hour in front of his classmates. But no matter how much the priests discipline him, Wilfrid already knows he's not going to become a priest. His dream job? To be a lawyer.

Coming out as a rebel

When Wilfrid returned from his two-year stay in New Glasgow, there still was no school in St-Lin for boys his age. Because he loved school and was such a bright kid, his father, Carolus, and Maman Adéline decided they'd just have to do with less and send him to a school where he could continue his studies. They saved up to pay the hefty fee for a college 32 kilometres east of St-Lin. And so, in September 1854, 13-year-old Wilfrid left St-Lin again. Although he looked forward to pursuing his studies, he did not realize just how much more strict life at his new school would be. In New Glasgow, he had been free to ramble in the woods and streams around the village. No such freedom would await him in l'Assomption.

Had his parents sent him to a dungeon?

Le Collège de l'Assomption had been established by the Catholic Church in 1832. Its mission was to prepare boys to become priests. It was a large, forbidding two-storey stone building divided into three different wings. When Wilfrid first entered its vast, dark corridors, he suddenly felt very small...and very scared. He wondered: had his parents sent him to study in a dungeon?

The priests at the Collège were strict and demanding, and kept Wilfrid on a tight schedule. Every day he had to get up at 5:25 a.m. and dress in a blue cloth uniform with a blue sash. After morning prayers, he went to study hall, then to Mass, and finally to a quick breakfast. Then he was off to classes where he studied Latin, Greek, the **classics** (like Virgil and Homer), French literature, philosophy, history, religion, and some English. With all that studying to do, Wilfrid hoped he would at least get his own desk. But instead of desks, the school provided long wooden doors placed atop sawhorses. The students studied near

1854
Wilfrid enrolls at Collège de l'Assomption.

1855
Wilfrid's sister, Malvina, dies of tuberculosis.

1857
Ottawa becomes the capital of the Province of Canada.

1861
Wilfrid graduates from college at l'Assomption.

1861
Wilfrid moves to Montreal and begins taking classes at McGill University.

1861
Wilfrid meets Zoé Lafontaine and begins courting her.

1864
Wilfrid graduates from McGill and is called to the bar of Canada East (now Quebec).

15

Getting the Church out of politics was one of Wilfrid's favourite causes, even as a young student.

It was his chosen topic as part of the debating team he'd organized at *Collège de l'Assomption...*

But the priests were so angry with him that they shut down the debating team soon afterward!

wood-burning stoves and used oil lamps for reading. When Wilfrid was thirsty, there was no water fountain to be found. He had to go to a small pond out back to get his drinking water! His busy routine left little time for playing, but, due to his poor health, Wilfrid couldn't take part in sports anyway. In his free time he preferred to wander in the woods or stay in bed and read.

Ending up with sore knees

On his very first day, Wilfrid was told by his English teacher that everyone had to study hard or be thrown out of the Collège. Then that same teacher announced that there would be no going home for the holidays. Wilfrid's heart sank. Another one of his coughing fits struck and he thought he might be dying because of his family's history of consumption, but his teacher just ignored him!

With this rigid training Wilfrid could have easily become a priest, but he knew early on that he didn't want that kind of life. He met several members of the **Parti rouge**, a political group, while living in l'Assomption. All of them were lawyers and all of them made a deep impression on the idealistic Wilfrid. He often skipped classes to slip into the courthouse behind the Collège and eavesdrop. The result? VERY sore knees! As punishment for breaking Collège rules, he was forced to kneel for an hour ("*À genoux!*" his teacher commanded) in front of the whole school. Still, he knew he'd found his dream job. "That's me!" he told his friends when he saw a lawyer defending a case in court. He knew then that he just had to study law at McGill University in Montreal and become a lawyer himself.

Heading out to university

After seven long years at the Collège, in the fall of 1861 Wilfrid finally moved to Montreal, where he boarded with family friends, Phoebé Gauthier and her doctor husband, Séraphin. They had several other lodgers and one of them just happened to be a beautiful piano teacher named **Zoé Lafontaine**. On his first day of classes, as he caught a transport car from his room at 25 Saint Louis Street then walked across the McGill campus, Wilfrid must have felt a whopping great sense of accomplishment. He had only begun formal schooling at age 11, and yet here he was, attending law school! And sure as heck nobody was going to yell "*À genoux!*" at him now! He must have caught a few of the ladies' eyes that day. At 20, he was a tall (over six feet), good-looking man, though extremely thin. He had a boyish face, bright eyes, full lips, and slightly curly chestnut hair. He carried himself proudly, and though he wore rough, country-made clothing, he was said to have the manners of a gentleman. He went to social events in Montreal and began courting (dating) the talented Zoé Lafontaine. He loved watching her lead groups of visiting people in singalongs. She even shared a sense of loss with Wilfrid: her mother had also died when she was young. He couldn't help but fall in love with her. They spent all their free time with each other and often spoke about their future together.

Wilfrid is a tall and handsome young man with a boyish face, bright eyes, full lips, and slightly curly chestnut hair. He wears rough, country-made clothing but carries himself proudly and has the manners of a gentleman.

1861

Wilfrid can't help falling in love with Zoé. The two of them spend all their free time with each other, often traveling across Montreal in the country's first tramway system.

The Catholic Church wants to keep things as they are. To do this, it aligns itself with the interests of rich and influential people in Quebec. Anyone who challenges that goal is labelled a threat to Canadian society.

"There is here now no other family than the human family, whatever the language they speak or the altars at which they kneel."

Wilfrid is seen as a troublemaker because he refuses to give in to pressure from the Church. Having fine-tuned his grasp of the law at McGill University, he quickly learns to uses his eloquence and charisma to convince people of his ideas. He argues for the separation of Church and State, and the freedom for people to vote according to their personal beliefs.

Turning red

Wilfrid studied hard to become a lawyer but still attended political events whenever possible. Soon he became a well-known member of the Parti rouge in Montreal. At that time in Canada, there was a great rivalry between the Parti rouge and another political group, the **Parti bleu**.

To understand the situation, think of each group as rival hockey teams. The blue team (*les bleus*) was made up of the Catholic clergy in Quebec and the pro-British Anglicans of English Canada (they later made up the **Conservative Party of Canada**). Since les bleus mostly represented the rich and influential people of the country, they generally wanted to keep things as they were. The other team, the reds (*les rouges*), were mostly French Canadians who teamed up with non-British Protestant groups. They were in favour of personal freedom and wanted to keep the Church out of politics. Their team joined the **Reform party** of Upper Canada, which later changed its name to the **Liberal Party of Canada**. (See the box on page 21 to find out more about this.)

1866
Wilfrid moves to the village of L'Avenir and becomes editor of the radical newspaper *Le Défricheur*.

1866
Several Fenian raids take place on the border with the United States.

1867
The Canadian Confederation takes effect on July 1.

1867
Wilfrid moves to Arthabaskaville and starts a law practice.

1868
Wilfrid marries Zoé Lafontaine.

1870
The Northwest Territories and Manitoba are created from Rupert's Land.

1870
Louis Riel leads the Red River Rebellion.

1871
Wilfrid is elected to the National Assembly in Quebec.

1871
Wilfrid is elected to National Assembly as a member of the Liberal party.

Heaven is blue and hell is red

Right before elections, parish priests would tell their congregations: "*Le ciel est bleu, et l'enfer est rouge!*" ("Heaven is blue and hell is red!") This warning implied that rouges people like Wilfrid and those who supported people like him would be going straight to hell for their actions! It was the Church leaders' way of trying to influence people against voting for rouges candidates. The Church considered the Parti rouge a "menace to society" because they were "independent thinkers." Because of such warnings, Liberals like Wilfrid and his rouges friends were considered by many Catholics to be dangerously rebellious. As a result, it was more difficult for rouges candidates to get elected.

After graduating, Wilfrid worked hard at an exciting job with a Montreal law firm. In 1866, he became sick. Something was seriously wrong with his lungs. The doctors thought he had tuberculosis.

Always ahead of his time

Zoé wanted to marry Wilfrid right after he graduated. But how could he marry? He was convinced he would die from his illness. Though it broke his heart, his sickness forced him to leave Zoé, whom he told to date other men. He moved to the country, to a town called Arthabaskaville, hoping it would be easier for him to breathe. It was there that he became involved with les rouges and won the job of editing a rouges newspaper. The priests, of course, ordered people not to read his paper, so it failed financially. Wilfrid was even thrown out of the nearby Catholic parish for his writings. (He had been writing that the priests should not tell people who to vote for or against. See the box on the separation of Church and State, page 21.) This forced Wilfrid to stick to being a lawyer and start his own law practice. Soon there he was again, overworked and overtired and starting to feel absolutely rotten, when, one night in May 1868, he received a telegram from Dr. Gauthier, his former landlord. The doctor told him to come to Montreal at once! Something serious had to be resolved!

A speedy engagement

Wilfrid knew in his heart that the telegram was about Zoé. He rushed to Montreal by train, arriving at the Gauthier's house early the next day. Dr. Gauthier promptly examined him, then pronounced that Wilfrid didn't have tuberculosis after all! He had chronic bronchitis, unpleasant but definitely not deadly. What a relief this was to Wilfrid. Furthermore, the doctor insisted that bronchitis was no reason not to marry.

"Don't you love Zoé?" he said. "Of course I do, but isn't she engaged to marry someone else?" Wilfrid asked.

Talk about cramping your style! In Wilfrid's time, the Catholic Church would forbid people from reading any books it did not approve of!

Wilfrid himself had about 5,000 books in his library. How many of those do you think the Church would have liked?

The wall of separation between Church and State

Human beings have fought and died over their religious and political differences for thousands of years. Can keeping religion and politics separate from one another prevent wars? Many people think so. They also believe it can protect human rights, including the right to freedom of (or from) religion.

The mixing of religion and politics has been a factor in many wars throughout history: the Crusades, the Huguenot Wars, the Thirty Years' War, the French and Russian revolutions. What sparked them? Oppression. Injustice. An intolerance of other religions. A concentration of so much power between church and government that common people were exploited and suppressed—citizens wanting the freedom to elect the government that they thought would govern them best, not one appointed by a church or monarchy claiming a divine right to rule.

Many Europeans immigrated to North America to avoid religious persecution by their own governments. Puritans, Quakers, Amish, Doukhobors, and Jews all fled unjust laws, intolerance, and violence in their home countries. And while the world has changed in many ways, countries that outlaw all religion or force their citizens to practise one state religion still exist today.

America's founders didn't want a repeat of history's holy wars and persecutions, so the principle that governments should maintain a neutral attitude toward religion was born. It began with a bill written by US president Thomas Jefferson in 1777, which guaranteed freedom of, and from, religion. "Religion is a matter which lies solely between man and his God," he wrote.

Wilfrid supported Jefferson's "wall of separation" between politics and religion, but it was a shaky wall in Canada during his lifetime. Imagine asking God to not send your parents to hell for voting for a candidate the Church disapproves of! In Wilfrid's time, that's what the Catholic clergy ordered kids to do—and they said the same to wives should their husbands vote the "wrong" way.

Today, thanks to the **Canadian Charter of Rights and Freedoms**, the government keeps religion separate from its policy-making. This guarantees rights such as access to public education without religion, books and media without censorship, birth control, and, most recently, same-sex marriage. People are still free to live by the rules of their faith, but the law says they get to choose for themselves.

In the United States, some people believe that an ultra-conservative administration under President George W. Bush is removing the wall of separation between Church and State. Because of the dominance of American culture on the rest of the world, we can expect more heated debate over issues like the war on terrorism, same-sex marriage, sex education, birth control, abortion, and religion in public education.

So do you think we've learned from our history, or is history repeating itself?

For more information about Church and State, visit our website at www.jackfruitpress.com.

In October 1877, the Quebec Catholic clergy received a letter from the Pope's office in Rome.

It forbade bishops from speaking for or against a political party. Priests were forbidden to teach about the sinfulness of voting for any one party, and were never to give their personal opinions from the pulpit.

Modern Catholicism is more accepting of others' opinions, and often participates in multi-faith events and memorial services.

With Wilfrid's love for Zoé confirmed, Wilfrid proposed formally and she accepted. Zoé told him they should get married that very day. Wilfrid hesitated, but she was really fed up with waiting for him and stubbornly insisted that they get married right away. So they did! That very same day!

Facing off with the Bishop

In 1871, Wilfrid ran for election as a Liberal (the rouges' new name) member of the Quebec legislature. He'd earned himself quite the reputation for speaking out about how the clergy should not interfere in politics.

The Catholic clergy warned their followers against voting for someone as radical as Wilfrid. One bishop used a local newspaper column to attack him almost weekly. His comments were so aggressive and malicious that they made Zoé cry and she feared the ferocity of the election campaign would kill Wilfrid. It almost did: throughout the campaign he was shivering with fever, coughing blood, and having difficulty breathing.

Fighting his ill-health every step of the way, Wilfrid refused to give up. In fact, people were impressed by his energetic campaign. He was an eloquent public speaker who was uniquely gifted when it came to swaying others with his words. The newspaper *Le Pays* (the *Country*) wrote "What an orator!" and "For the first time in years, we heard a speech based upon principles." What had Wilfrid said to evoke such praise, you ask? That no matter what the Catholic Church told them to do, the people of Quebec should be allowed to vote however they wanted. And guess what? They didn't just listen, they voted exactly the way they wanted! He was elected! Many Catholics voted for him after all. So did English-speaking Protestants. However, he was the only Liberal candidate elected in the whole province.

Sticking to his principles

It didn't take long for Wilfrid to make an impression in the **Quebec Assembly**. He vigorously argued against the system of dual representation. This system allowed a government representative to work for a provincial and a federal government at the same time. Wilfrid opposed this because it encouraged politicians to mix federal issues with provincial ones. His motion was rejected at first . . . but then, with a bit of time, others started to agree with him . . . and by 1873, ministers who worked for the province were no longer allowed to work for the federal government. He'd learned his lessons about sticking to his task, and sticking to his principles. He would soon apply those same lessons to the work he did in Ottawa.

Wilfrid has earned himself quite the reputation for speaking out about how the clergy should NOT be interfering in politics. But the battle is intense. The Church fights back at every step.

1871

"I must do this, Zoé. I am entering public life without any desire except to make my ideas triumph."

Zoé fears that the election campaign will kill Wilfrid. It almost does: throughout the campaign, Wilfrid shivers with fever, coughs up blood, and has difficulty breathing. Still, he refuses to give up and continues campaigning.

1875

During his exile, Louis Riel, leader of the failed <u>Red River Rebellion</u>, secretly hides away in Quebec. One night, Laurier is invited to the village priest's house for dinner, where he is surprised to see Riel.

At first, Wilfrid is impressed that Riel is well informed about politics. But when Riel starts talking about his special mission to reveal God's will, Wilfrid thinks he's crazy. In spite of that, Wilfrid remains committed to defending Riel's right to take up arms against injustice.

Standing up for his principles

1874
Wilfrid is elected as a member of Parliament.

1875
The Supreme Court of Canada is established.

Laurier meets Louis Riel.

1877
Wilfrid becomes minister of inland revenue in **Alexander Mackenzie**'s government.

1878
The Liberal party is defeated by the Conservatives. Wilfrid resigns his cabinet post and wins the Quebec East seat in the next election.

1885
The Northwest Rebellion takes place. Louis Riel is executed.

1887
Wilfrid becomes leader of the federal Liberal party and leader of the Opposition.

1891
John Abbott becomes prime minister.

1892
Sir John Thompson becomes prime minister.

1894
Sir Mackenzie Bowell becomes prime minister.

1896
Sir Charles Tupper becomes prime minister.

Wilfrid became a Liberal member of Parliament in February 1874. It would be a long and winding road to the position of prime minister. And the greatest roadblock Wilfrid faced was himself. It's easy to assume that people who "make it" have everything going for them, but, in reality, Wilfrid had always suffered from either self-doubt or a lack of energy due to his chronic bronchitis. In fact, he nearly didn't become a politician at all. When a federal seat became vacant, his friends had to convince him to run in the 1874 election!

Wilfrid had taken on a law partner, Joseph Lavergne, in 1874, and his law business succeeded so well that Wilfrid earned enough money to hire an architect and have a country home built in Arthabaskaville. When it was finished in 1877, it was a grand brick house built at the foot of Mount Arthabaska. It became Wilfrid and Zoé's refuge, their favourite place to relax and entertain friends.

Feeling lonely in Ottawa

When he first arrived in Ottawa to attend Parliament, Wilfrid felt achingly lonely. Zoé had stayed home in Arthabaskaville and he missed her company tremendously. Compared to the other confident, outgoing MPs around him, he felt small. He even gave his first speech in the **House of Commons** in French to help overcome his shyness. But most of the other MPs didn't even pay attention.

Wilfrid's first speech in English, in April 1874, argued against exiling **Métis** leader **Louis Riel** from Canada. He reminded the House of the love of justice and fair play that he had learned from the British. Riel and his followers, he said, had only wanted to be treated as British subjects and not "bartered away like common cattle." Where is the act of rebellion in that? he asked. Although they still voted to boot Riel out of Canada for five years, the other MPs admired Wilfrid's speech.

The finest speech ever pronounced

Like anything in life, however, practice makes perfect. Wilfrid's political speeches eventually got better—actually, much better. In March 1886, he delivered an English speech that Liberal party leader **Edward Blake** called "the finest speech ever pronounced in the Parliament of Canada since **Confederation**." The speech supported a motion against Prime Minister **John A. Macdonald** and his government because that government had permitted the November 1885 hanging of Louis Riel.

When Wilfrid stood up in the House and defended the rights of the Métis, many politicians—Conservative and Liberal alike—began to look at him differently. Suddenly, he seemed like the kind of man who had the courage to speak up and lead a party. Perhaps he could one day lead the country. Edward Blake knew then and there that Wilfrid would eventually follow in his footsteps to become leader of the Liberal Party of Canada.

He too would have fought in the rebellion

Wilfrid never held back when speaking against the government's unfair treatment of the Métis. In an earlier speech, just after Riel's execution, he told a giant protest rally in Montreal, "Had I been born on the banks of the Saskatchewan, I myself would have shouldered a musket to fight against the neglect of governments and the shameless greed of speculators." He would have fought in Riel's **Northwest Rebellion**! This controversial comment shocked many English Canadians but Laurier didn't care. He would remain loyal to his ideals and his belief in the rights of ordinary men no matter what anyone else thought.

I think I can...but can I?

While Wilfrid delivered passionate speeches in the House of Commons, he often let his insecurities get the better of him. He was dogged by the feeling that he lacked the experience to get to the next step: to

Louis Riel was a Métis lawyer who led two armed rebellions against the Canadian government. Riel was defending the rights and lands of the French, Métis and First Nations people of the territories that later became Manitoba and Saskatchewan.

become leader of his party. As a result, his career seemed at a stand-still from the early to mid-1880s. To many people, he appeared to lack both ambition and energy. A reporter in the press gallery at the House of Commons reported that many other members of his party were starting to believe that Laurier's political career was finished.

Wilfrid never holds back when speaking against the government's unfair treatment of the Métis. In one speech, just after Riel's execution, he addresses a giant protest rally in Montreal.

1885

"Had I been born on the banks of the Saskatchewan, I myself would have shouldered a musket to fight against the neglect of governments and the shameless greed of speculators."

Wilfrid makes it clear the he would have fought in Riel's rebellion! This controversial comment shocks many English Canadians. But Wilfrid is determined to remain loyal to his ideals and his belief in the rights of ordinary people no matter what anyone else thinks.

Was choosing Laurier a blunder?

Wilfrid took over leadership of Canada's Liberal party on June 18, 1887. Since the Conservatives were now in power, Wilfrid became leader of the loyal Opposition. Not only was he surrounded by plenty of naysayers but he clearly didn't believe he could stand up to the infighting and verbal slugfests this job demanded. In a letter home to his wife, he confessed "I know I have not the aptitude for it, and I have a sad apprehension that it must end in disaster."

One member of the Liberal party believed that the choice of Laurier as leader of the party was a "fearful blunder"; another worried about his lack of physical strength. Then, during Wilfrid's first Ontario tour as Liberal leader, in the summer of 1887, a longtime member of the Liberal party whispered to a reporter that "Laurier will never make a leader; he has not enough of the Devil in him."

Time turned out to be the best healer for Wilfrid's lack of self-confidence. He spent more time speaking in front of crowds, and, with each new session in the House of Commons, he became a more charismatic speaker and forceful debater. He also grew healthier and stronger with every summer visit back to what he thought of as his oasis, his home in Arthabaskaville.

Shaking hands with tens of thousands of people

Between 1894 and the election that would make him prime minister, in 1896, Wilfrid likely shook hands with tens of thousands of voters in the West. Why so many? He wanted to meet the people of western Canada, since he was representing them as Liberal leader. But he also suspected that those in the West were more likely to vote for a Catholic French Canadian who spoke perfect English with a slight Scottish accent than for any member of the Conservative party, because the Conservatives hadn't helped them out in the past. He was right!

Do you really have to be "devilish" to be a successful politician? Some would say you do. Laurier certainly would not have agreed. He was polite, acted like a gentleman, and never hurled insults at his opponents.

Some feel that mudslinging actually hurts politics and makes voters distrust governments and disrespect politicians. What do you think?

As leader of the Opposition, Laurier is surrounded by plenty of naysayers. He clearly doubts he can measure up to the infighting and verbal slugfests this job demands.

1887

"I have accepted leadership, but I am convinced of my shortcomings ... I find no pleasure in it and the fact is that I have not the financial means."

During Wilfrid's first Ontario tour as Liberal leader, a long-time member of the Liberal party whispers to a reporter that "Laurier will never make a leader; he has not enough of the Devil in him."

A massive victory parade takes place the very next day after Wilfrid's election as Canada's first French-Canadian prime minister. It is the largest celebration Quebec city has ever seen. Everyone is there to cheer him on.

The secret of the future

Wilfrid Laurier became the first French-Canadian prime minister of Canada on June 23, 1896, at the age of 54. At last, French Quebec had a leader in the House. He was one of theirs—a French Catholic— and an eloquent speaker, and they loved him for it.

What a parade they had!

What a victory parade there was that night! A carriage filled with flowers took Zoé and the new prime minister through the streets of Quebec City, which were decorated with flags and large pictures of Wilfrid. Hundreds of people lined the streets, bands played—and there was

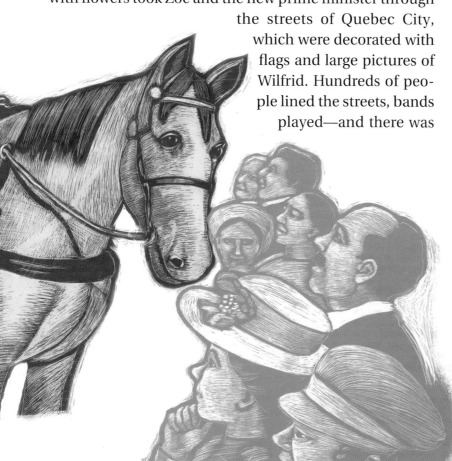

1896
Wilfrid is elected the seventh prime minister of Canada.

He works out a settlement for the Manitoba Schools Act.

1897
Wilfrid is knighted.

Queen Victoria celebrates her diamond jubilee.

The Klondike gold rush takes place.

1898
The Yukon Territory is formed.

1899
Wilfrid refuses to send Canadian troops to fight in South Africa during the Boer War.

1900
Wilfrid creates the national Department of Labour.

1901
Queen Victoria dies.

Edward VII becomes the King of England.

Guglielmo Marconi receives the first transatlantic wireless radio transmission in St. John's, NFLD.

1902
The Boer War ends.

1904
Wilfrid speaks to the Canadian Club of Ottawa.

Queen Victoria had a secret reason for knighting Wilfrid.

In 1897, Great Britain was trying to exert more control over the affairs of its colonies.

The Brits thought that if they buttered up Wilfrid, he'd convince Canada and the other colonies to strengthen their ties to the empire.

But Wilfrid was more interested in keeping Canada strong and independent!

even a fireworks display. Then, to Wilfrid's surprise, some young men who had voted for him unhitched his horses, lifted up his carriage, and carried it on their shoulders through the crowd as everyone yelled "Hurrah!" But not everybody was happy with his victory. A Toronto newspaper editor wrote that the country had been sold to the French. Wilfrid would do his best to prove his critics wrong. Long ago, Wilfrid had said that the secret of the future lay in the union of the people. He was now to be given the chance to make that union better.

Becoming a "Sir"

To celebrate **Queen Victoria**'s diamond jubilee (her 60th year as Queen) in 1897, Wilfrid and his wife were invited to England. They received the honour of riding first in the procession—right after the Queen's carriage—because Canada was the most important country in the **Commonwealth**. Wilfrid attended many banquets, gave dozens of speeches, and was given **honourary degrees** from both Oxford and Cambridge Universities. Finally, the Queen invited him to Windsor Castle and Buckingham Palace, where he was knighted Sir Wilfrid Laurier, member of the Privy Council.

Despite the new powers that gave him a sharper confidence and authority, Sir Wilfrid's personality stayed warm and friendly. He did his best to keep in touch with the ordinary people of Canada, a nation that was changing in attitudes and culture with every passing year. The country boy who used to wear rough clothing had become an aristocratic gentleman in Ottawa, always impeccably dressed in the latest fashion, with beautiful manners. A tall, handsome, kindly person who had time to smile and exchange pleasant talk, he had become one of the most loved and respected prime ministers that Canada has ever had.

The compromises begin: Manitoba's school question

When Manitoba joined Confederation in 1870, most of its population was made up of French, Métis, and First Nations people. This soon changed. The **Canadian Pacific Railway** made it easy for English-speaking settlers to move into the area and they did, forcing the Métis off their land. The number of French-language settlers dwindled and soon they were few in number, while the number of English-speaking people steadily increased. The government of Manitoba decided it did not make sense to maintain French schools so they stopped funding them. Manitoba also abolished French as an official language of the province.

This angered Canada's French population. Since the Conservative Party seemed to support Manitoba's decision Quebec's voters, who had been voting overwhelmingly for the Conservatives, switched their support to Sir Wilfrid's Liberal party. The School Question, as it was called, was the primary issue of the 1896 election and Sir Wilfrid's promise of a good solu-

Invited to England to celebrate Queen Victoria's diamond jubilee, Wilfrid and his wife enjoy a special honour. Because Canada is seen as the most important country in the Commonwealth, their carriage is right behind the Queen's.

Magnificently dressed in fine clothes, Wilfrid is proud to be dubbed "Sir Wilfrid" by the Queen. Some of his French-speaking colleagues feel he should reject a British title, but Wilfrid wants the honour. He also thinks it might improve his personal prestige with English-speaking voters.

tion gained him the support he needed to win that election and become prime minister. It was at this time that he earned his nickname, "The Great Conciliator," for his talent at reaching compromises with his opponents. Sir Wilfrid managed to make relations between the country's English Protestants and French Catholics more peaceful—for a while.

Saying no to the Boer War

In 1899, war broke out between the Boers (Dutch settlers) of South Africa and the British, who were colonizing Africa. When Britain asked Canada to send troops, Sir Wilfrid ignored the request. Later, he explained that his government would not contribute troops because there was "no menace to Canada." This did not please those people who felt that Canada had a duty to defend the interests of the **British Empire**. They demanded that Wilfrid resign. Rather than resigning, he offered to come up with *une voie moyenne*—a compromise. His solution? He refused to force Canadians to fight and would not send the 10,000 troops that Britain had asked for. However, his government offered to pay the costs of men who volunteered to fight. He also made sure that the British government understood that this decision did not mean Canada would always help them fight their wars.

Creating a Department of Labour

With the wonderful promise of land, wheat, and money in the late 1890s, immigrants also came to mine for minerals. In 1896, the year Sir Wilfrid became prime minister, prospectors began rushing north to find gold in the **Klondike**.

Canada's population was growing and there was work to be done, but with that work came long hours, poor pay, and many dangers for workers in the mines and factories. To keep family incomes large enough to survive, women and even children had to take jobs, though the work they could get only paid a pittance. A man's average wage was $7 a week. Women made up 20 per cent of the workforce in 1896, and children (as young as five or six years old) made up 4 per cent!

By the turn of the century, a working "boom" took place in industries like mining and lumber, putting even more pressure on the workforce. That's why Sir Wilfrid set up Canada's first Department of Labour in 1900: to create labour laws that would help settle arguments between workers and their bosses, and hopefully improve working conditions for Canadians.

Immigration's impact on Canada

As the 20th century arrived, Canada's economic climate quickly changed from one of struggle to one of prosperity. Taking advantage of that change, Laurier's cabinet took over Canada's economic development with great energy. One member from Manitoba, **Clifford Sifton** (minister of the interior from 1896 to 1905), had himself been a successful farmer. Building on his own experience, he wanted skilled farmers emigrating to Canada, families who knew how to grow wheat in the challenging climate of the Prairies.

Armed with posters that proclaimed Canada's Prairies to be "The Last Best West," Sifton's agents went to Britain and the US, then Austria-Hungary, Russia, and the Ukraine. Their efforts worked. Starting with a trickle at first, the number of people coming to Canada grew from 20,000 in 1896 to 190,000 in 1906. By 1911, over a million people had settled on the Prairies. New towns grew up as fast as the campsites they replaced. New rail lines opened up lands to more settlers, more towns. The population of the country grew from 4,833,000 in 1891 to 7,207,000 in 1911!

Life was hard for the early settlers. Most got off the ships with only their clothes and tools. Although immigration agents were instructed to discourage Asians, Blacks, Italians, and Jews, many came anyway. For instance, 138,000 Jews arrived between 1900-1921 as refugees from religious persecution in Eastern Europe and Russia. Not all immigrants were farmers. Thousands of skilled factory workers and their families were needed by new industries in the cities. They flocked to jobs that might be there one day but gone the next, as new inventions altered production. City populations grew at about the same rate as towns in the West. Crowding was the rule as whole families lived in one or two rooms. No work meant starvation. In Montreal slums, 34 people out of every thousand died from illness linked to poverty.

The face of Canada changed and so did its people. English, French, and German Canadians used to their own language found themselves surrounded by many other languages. There was now a greater need for unity and tolerance, for goodwill and understanding. Canada was changing from a single culture to a diverse society, combining many new languages and peoples. Canadians (old and new) were delighted at their country's new prosperity, its unique beauty, its power, its awesome size, and its many natural treasures and resources.

Immigrants line up for medical examinations (circa 1890–1910)

For more information about immigration, visit our website at www.jackfruitpress.com.

1910

Canada's population and economy are growing rapidly. By 1903, the CPR no longer meets the needs of the country. Sir Wilfrid approves the construction of a new Canadian transcontinental railway.

"I hope you will grow up to be a great man someday."

Eager to explore Canada himself, Sir Wilfrid goes on several trips across the country. In 1910, on a stopover in Saskatoon, he meets a young newspaper vendor named John Diefenbaker. This boy proudly tells the PM that he too intends to be prime minister of Canada one day. And he will...47 years later.

Building the nation

As Sir Wilfrid's career reached its peak, Canada (and the whole continent of North America) happened to be undergoing a period of prosperity, growth, and change like no other before. Rising to the occasion, Sir Wilfrid took charge of things with a confidence and an aplomb that had not been seen in the actions of any previous prime minister.

A new transcontinental railway

By 1903, the Canadian Pacific Railway was no longer adequate to meet the needs of the nation; there was more wheat to ship than it could carry. Sir Wilfrid gave his nod of approval for the construction of a new Canadian transcontinental railway. Another influx of immigrant workers provided manpower to build this new railway and to populate new towns growing up along the railway lines.

Two new provinces

The next step for Canada, the creation of new provinces, seemed only natural. Under Sir Wilfrid's government, Alberta and Saskatchewan were created in 1905 from territories that Canada had purchased from the **Hudson's Bay Company**. People living in these territories had been wanting them to become provinces for a while. Becoming a province meant that citizens of that territory would now have the right to vote and a say in how they would be

1903
Wilfrid gets construction started on a second Canadian transcontinental railway.

1905
Wilfrid creates the provinces of Alberta and Saskatchewan, which join Confederation.

1909
Wilfrid founds the Department of External Affairs.

1910
Wilfrid creates the Royal Canadian Navy, passing The Naval Service Bill.

1911
Wilfrid is defeated by Sir Robert Laird Borden in the federal election.

He becomes Opposition leader.

1914
World War I begins.

1917
A conscription crisis occurs.

Canadian soldiers fight the Battle of Vimy Ridge in France.

1918
World War I ends.

Women are allowed to vote in all but two provinces.

1919
Wilfrid dies on February 17. He is buried in Notre Dame Cemetery in Ottawa.

During an open air speech in Edmonton, Wilfrid spotted a young girl in the crowd.

She was leaning dangerously from an upper floor window in a building across the street.

Interrupting his speech, Wilfrid pointed at the girl and asked, "Is that little one safe?"

He waited until she was safe before returning to his speech. Though he lost the election that followed, people never forgot this incident because it showed just how much he cared about people.

governed. Sir Wilfrid's election promise led to the formation of these new provinces from the remapping of the Northwest Territories. Confederation expanded once again, as the two new provincial governments sent their elected representatives to Ottawa.

New watchdogs on government

Before Sir Wilfrid intervened, all kinds of favours, profitable government jobs, and contracts were given only to friends and relatives of politicians. This was happening in many government departments. Some members of Parliament even tried to buy their way into becoming knights. Sir Wilfrid was not personally involved in any of these dealings and very much opposed them. He believed that the Canadian government needed a fair method for handing out jobs and contracts. He urged the creation of the Federal Civil Service Commission in 1907. This organization was formed to ensure that anyone who worked for the government was qualified instead of just being recommended by their local politician. He also promoted a Committee of Natural Resources to check on wastage in fisheries, mines, forests, and water by careless developers. This was the first step ever undertaken by the Canadian government to protect the country's environment.

Struggling for a say in agreements

Another situation that troubled Sir Wilfrid was the "Alaskan question." After the United States bought Alaska from Russia in the 1860s, American use of the Pacific coast had crept down the shores of British Columbia to include more and more of the coastline. The Klondike gold rush in the Yukon made it obvious that the Yukon could benefit greatly from having its own seaport.

Concerned that Canada might lose access to the Pacific Ocean, Wilfrid's government asked for the situation to be settled by an unbiased committee. The committee chosen to make a decision on the matter was made up of six judges: three Americans, two Canadians and one Briton.

After much discussion, the committee decided in favour of the United States. The British judge sided with the Americans because Britain wanted to keep good relations with America. Canada was still just a colony and could do nothing but accept the result. This made Sir Wilfrid even more determined that Canada no longer be a colony without any clout. In 1909, he created the Department of External Affairs to give Canada the power to make its own treaties and settle its own disputes.

Some of his party members opposed the new motion. Sir Wilfrid showed them how strongly he felt about it by writing out his letter of resignation! This caused many of his party to change their minds. They didn't want to

Language rights have been a hot issue for a long time. When Ontario's Regulation 17 tries to restrict the rights of French-speaking children to be taught in their language, Sir Wilfrid steps into the debate.

"I want every child in Ontario to benefit from an English education. Would you deny my countrymen in Ontario the right also to be educated in their [French] tongue?"

In a speech about cultural tolerance, Sir Wilfrid insists that the government restore the children's language privileges.

lose their leader over the issue—and they didn't. Sir Wilfrid stayed on as leader of the Opposition until he died.

A navy of kitchen pots?

Another way Sir Wilfrid helped Canada gain its independence was by building the country's first fleet of ships. The Naval Service Bill declared that a navy be built and that men volunteer to serve in this new Royal Canadian Navy. Politicians at the time laughed and called it a "tin-pot navy," comparing it to the huge British fleet. The government had enough money to build only a few ships at first.

In fact, few people were happy with the decision. French Canadians thought the navy was simply another way to fight England's wars, which they most definitely did not want to do. And English Canadians didn't think it was good enough, and enjoyed poking fun at it!

Fear of trade with the United States

On a tour during his 1910 election campaign, Sir Wilfrid took the transcontinental railway he'd helped create through Winnipeg, Saskatoon, Regina, Moose Jaw, Edmonton, Calgary, Banff, Victoria, and Prince Rupert. Thousands of citizens came to the railway stations to meet him and attend his speeches. One day his colleagues found him alone at a railway station playing ball with a child.

Sir Wilfrid felt loved by the Canadian people, but he didn't realize that he wasn't as in tune with their wants as he had been in the past. During the election, he proposed a free-trade policy (called the Reciprocity Treaty) with the United States, which he believed could only lead to greater prosperity for Canada. Instead, it led to his own defeat.

Until then, American goods that competed with similar products made in Canada were taxed. This tax (or "tariff," as it was known) made the foreign goods more expensive. This allowed Canadian industries to compete with American industries who could usually manufacture the same goods more cheaply and sell them at a lower price in Canada. Under Reciprocity, Canada would agree to reduce these tariffs. Americans could then sell their goods at a cheaper price than most Canadians manufacturer could.

Canada's financial leaders—bankers and business people and the like—were afraid that a trade deal with the US would hurt Canada economically. Sir Wilfrid's Liberal party also misjudged the public's mood, not seeing that miners, farmers, and lumber merchants feared they might lose their jobs because of the deal. **Sir Robert Borden**'s Conservatives, who had campaigned heavily against free trade, won the election of 1911. Borden's criticism of the high cost of the Sir Wilfrid's unfinished railway and the "tin pot navy" had also contributed to Wilfrid's defeat.

Wilfrid thought that free trade would help Canada's bogged-down trade economy. He thought he knew the people's wishes, but the voters didn't agree, and voted the Liberals out of power.

Scandal! Read all about it!

It all began innocently enough: Wilfrid befriended Émilie Lavergne, the wife of Joseph, his friend and legal partner in Arthabaska, long before he became PM. Émilie was not beautiful. Actually, she was short and had crooked teeth! But Wilfrid found a kindred spirit in Émilie. She was intellectual—an avid reader like him—and they enjoyed conversing with each other and writing letters back and forth.

Some neighbours, acquaintances, and socialite gossips assumed that their friendship was a romance. And journalists wrote about this romance as if it were a proven fact. They even suggested Wilfrid was the father of Émilie's son, **Armand**, because the boy looked a lot like him! We may never know the truth.

Zoé dismissed these stories as pure rumours. She trusted Wilfrid and considered Émilie a good friend. That must not have been easy. It's difficult to hear rotten things being said about you or someone you love, whether they are true or not!

Armand Lavergne was rumoured to be Wilfrid's son

Perhaps that wasn't the best plan, because historians still wonder if the stories were true.

Long before Sir Wilfrid's time, people have enjoyed peering into the private lives of politicians, royalty, and entertainment stars. Why? One reason is that whatever happens to them— from breaking a toe to battling alcoholism—makes money for others by increasing talk-show ratings and selling tabloids, newspapers, magazines, and even tickets to those celebrities' movies.

That's why when Mary-Kate or Ashley Olsen go anywhere, reporters follow them like salivating dogs, their tails a-wagging. But more often than not, these photographers act less like puppies and more like full-grown pit bulls! In the last decade, celebrities have come to view the reporters as bullies, forcing them to make every private detail of their lives public. Sometimes, this even means putting them in danger. Many people believe reporters are partly responsible for the 1997 death of Diana, Princess of Wales, because they chased down her limousine and caused it to crash.

Have you ever been called names by kids in your school ("Loser!" "Wimp!")? It leaves you feeling cold, naked, and humiliated. Maybe you find the courage within yourself to speak out against what is being said about you. But maybe it just feels easier to pretend it's not happening.

That was pretty much Wilfrid's solution—to ignore the rumours as if he didn't hear them.

Some celebrities say that smiling for the cameras and answering inappropriate questions are the price they have to pay for fame. But should our prime ministers have to reveal everything about their private lives once they run for public office? Do they owe that to their citizens, or is it an invasion of their right to privacy?

What do you think?

For more information about scandals, visit our website at www.jackfruitpress.com.

French language for Ontario kids

A few years later, Sir Wilfrid had to confront another major issue. This one had to do with French-language rights. Regulation 17 (passed by the Ontario government) was restricting the French-language schools to early grades only. French-speaking Ontarians were up in arms over this measure. It meant their kids could no longer learn in French. Sir Wilfrid upheld their cause by insisting that Ontario restore the children's language privileges. He did this by giving a powerful speech about cultural tolerance in the House of Commons.

No conscription!

Sir Wilfrid didn't disappear from politics after losing to Robert Borden. In fact, he delighted in being quite the thorn in the side of the new prime minister, and delivered many powerful speeches as Opposition leader. Later, he and Borden became friends.

All of his life, Sir Wilfrid had been a pacifist (a person opposed to war and violence). Although he supported Robert Borden's efforts during World War I, he refused to support Borden's 1917 conscription bill—a law that would force Canadian men aged 18 and older to serve in the army during the war. As Opposition leader, Laurier insisted "There is to be no conscription in Canada."

French Canada fully supported Sir Wilfrid in this issue because they could see no sense in having their sons killed in a war being fought in faraway Europe. English Canadians had a totally different reaction. They were enraged that Sir Wilfrid opposed the bill—so enraged that in the 1917 election, they voted overwhelmingly against him and his party. The Liberals were defeated everywhere except in Quebec. In spite of this defeat, Sir Wilfrid remained in Parliament as Opposition leader until his death from a series of strokes on February 17, 1919.

A show of love and support

Sir Wilfrid's funeral was held in Ottawa on February 20, 1919. Thousands of Canadians came to honour him and thousands more lined the streets on that cold winter day to view his funeral procession. As a symbol of his extraordinary efforts to create harmony between French and English Canadians, two funeral speeches were given: one in French and one in English.

Sir Wilfrid's hometown of St-Lin asked that his body be buried there after his death. But Quebec City also made the same request. Sir Wilfrid, however, had never considered himself only French Canadian. "I am a Canadian first, last, and all the time!" To symbolize this, he was buried in Notre Dame Cemetery, in our nation's capital city, Ottawa.

When Zoé died, in 1921, she willed their Ottawa home, Laurier House, to future prime minister William Lyon Mackenzie King.

Sir Wilfrid has been a pacifist (a person opposed to war) all of his life. Although he supports Canada's war effort, he refuses to support conscription—a law that forces men aged 18 and older to go to war.

A campaign urging young men to enlist gets mixed reactions. English-speaking people are eager to go to war to defend the Empire. But French-speaking citizens refuse to participate. They see no sense in risking their lives in a war they feel has no bearing on them.

Sir Wilfrid's Canada:

*"For the solution
of the problems,
you have
a safe guide
if you remember
…love is better
than hate."*

Sir Wilfrid Laurier, 1919

Sir Wilfrid died a happy man. Because, as far as he was concerned, he lived to see his dream become true. Like him, all of us consider ourselves Canadian first—and the amazing thing about being Canadian is that it means each one of us gets to keep our own cultural ancestry, just the way Sir Wilfrid kept his.

"I am a Canadian" is something we can all say with pride, knowing that, in spite of some of our past mistakes, diversity and tolerance are deeply woven into our national identity.

In helping to build this multicultural country, Sir Wilfrid gave us more than just a national story. He also gave us his own life as a success story. He wasn't born rich, nor did he grow up with money or the right connections. He'd lost both his mother and his sister before he'd turned 15. He struggled with frail health and low self-esteem all his life. He started out with no more than you or I have—and maybe a whole lot less. So what made him different from the average kid in his village?

Something happened when he was just a little boy, listening spellbound to his mother telling tales of Canadian rebels and his father daring to stand up to Church authorities. It kept happening as he sneaked out of school to eavesdrop in the courthouse, fascinated by the lawyers and their fight for justice. And it was still happening when he was a man, arguing for greater tolerance, understanding, and unity in the country he so loved.

One of Sir Wilfrid's greatest strengths was his upfront personality. Unlike many other politicians, who favoured backroom deals and secret arrangements, he liked to handle problems in the open. Rather

"Canada's story has only just begun."

A tolerant, multicultural country

than avoid problems or pretend they didn't exist, Sir Wilfrid brought issues out in the open and discussed them freely. Thanks to him, Canada became a place where conflicts are settled with words, not guns.

While he did not completely solve all the issues Canada faced, he did deal with all of them head-on, as they happened. And he proposed simple, rational solutions that were usually quite good.

Sir Wilfrid left us much more than railroads, new policies, and new ministries. He left us a model for peacefully pursuing our lives while respecting our fellow Canadians. This model adds to the tapestry of Canada.

What was Sir Wilfrid's secret? What kept him going, even when he was scared, even when he was sick? An inner voice? His own spirit? The courage of his convictions? I don't know exactly what it was . . . but I do know that you have it too. And if you listen to what calls your heart and fires your passion the way Sir Wilfrid did, you'll make your own life extraordinary, just as he did. As a matter of fact, if he could reach out to you from this book—the way he once reached out to a boy selling newspapers on a train platform—I bet you can guess exactly what he would say. "I hope you grow up to be a great person someday!" You will. And then you'll do your part in making a great country even better.

Timeline: The life and times of Sir Wilfrid Laurier

YEAR	WILFRID'S LIFE	EVENTS IN CANADA AND THE WORLD
1841	Wilfrid is born in St-Lin, Canada East, on November 20.	The Queen sanctions the union of Upper and Lower Canada. Upper Canada's name is changed to Canada West. Lower Canada becomes Canada East. The Dawn Settlement is created in Canada West to provide refuge for former slaves from the United States.
1842		The Northeastern Boundary Dispute between New Brunswick and Maine is settled by the Webster-Ashburton Treaty. Construction of the first railway in Nova Scotia begins.
1843		Fort Victoria is built by Britain to strengthen its claim to Vancouver Island. The Cornwall and Chambly Canals are officially opened.
1844	Wilfrid's sister Malvina is born on January 23.	Construction of the first railway in New Brunswick begins.
1845		The second Welland Canal is officially opened.
1846		British prime minister Robert Peel announces Free Trade. This ends the old colonial trade system.
1847		The St. Lawrence Canal is completed.
1848	Wilfrid's mom, Marcelle Martineau, dies on March 7.	Responsible government is granted to the Province of Canada.
1849	Wilfrid's dad Carolus marries Adéline Éthier.	
1850		The Fugitive Slave Act is passed in the USA. This results in free and enslaved black peoples fleeing to British North America.
1852	Wilfrid is sent to school in New Glasgow, Canada East.	In Chatham, Canada West, Mary Ann Shadd Cary becomes the first woman in North America to become a newspaper editor.
1854	Wilfrid enrolls at Collège de l'Assomption.	Reciprocity begins between British North America and the United States. The Crimean War takes place in the Balkans and the Crimean Peninsula: Russia fights the Ottoman (Turkish) Empire and its allies (Britain, France, and Sardinia). Many soldiers die needlessly due to terrible hospital conditions before Florence Nightingale introduces modern nursing methods.
1855	Wilfrid's sister Malvina dies.	Bytown is renamed Ottawa.
1856		The second Opium War takes place: China fights Britain and France in an attempt to end the opium trade.
1857		Ottawa becomes the capital of the Province of Canada. The revolt of 1857: India fights for freedom from British rule. The issues are laws that keep Indians impoverished and British army violations of the religious customs of Hindu and Muslim soldiers.
1858		Second Anglo Chinese War.
1859		Abraham Shadd becomes the first black person elected to public office.

More on the life and times of Sir Wilfrid Laurier

YEAR	WILFRID'S LIFE	EVENTS IN CANADA AND THE WORLD
1860		Construction begins on the House of Commons. The Maori Wars begin: The Maori of New Zealand fight to keep their land from British settlers. Large areas of land are confiscated. causing permanent damage to Maori society. The American Civil War (until 1865): President Lincoln and the northern states want to abolish slavery. The southern states go to war against the North. The North wins and slavery is ended.
1861	Wilfrid begins to study law at McGill University. He meets future wife Zoé Lafontaine. He starts work in the office of Rodolphe Laflamme. He joins l'Institut Canadien.	
1864	Wilfrid graduates from McGill with a Bachelor of Civil Law degree and is called to the bar of Canada East.	
1866	Wilfrid falls ill. He moves to L'Avenir, Canada East and becomes editor of *Le Défricheur* (The Pioneer).	Several Fenian raids take place on the border with the United States.
1867		Canadian Confederation takes effect on July 1. John A. Macdonald becomes the first prime minister of Canada.
1868	Wilfrid and Zoé Lafontaine are married on May 18.	The first Federal Militia Act creates the first Canadian army.
1870		The Red River Rebellion takes place. Thomas Scott is executed by Louis Riel's provisional government. The Northwest Territories and Manitoba are created.
1871	Wilfrid is elected to the National Assembly in Quebec City as a member of the Liberal party.	British Columbia joins Confederation.
1872		The first nationwide labour protest is held. Asian and Native peoples are banned from voting in BC.
1873		Sir John A. Macdonald is forced to resign as prime minister because of the Pacific Scandal. Alexander Mackenzie becomes the second prime minister. The Northwest Mounted Police is formed.
1874	Wilfrid resigns from the National Assembly. He is elected as a member of Parliament.	Liberals win a majority government in the federal election of January 22.
1875		The Supreme Court of Canada is established. The Indian Act is passed.
1877	Wilfrid is appointed minister of inland revenue (1877-1878).	Manzo Nagano is the first official Japanese immigrant to Canada. The Russian-Turkish War begins: a continuation of a series of wars between Russia and the Ottoman Empire over land boundaries.

Still more on the life and times of Sir Wilfrid Laurier

YEAR	WILFRID'S LIFE	EVENTS IN CANADA AND THE WORLD
1878	The Liberal party is defeated by the Conservatives. Wilfrid loses his seat in the Quebec Assembly.	John A. Macdonald is elected for a second term as prime minister. The Canada Temperance Act is passed.
1879		The Anglo-Zulu War takes place in South Africa: Britain wins and takes over control of Zululand. The War of the Pacific begins: Peru, Bolivia, and Chile fight over borders and natural resources.
1880		Edward Hanlan, a rower, becomes Canada's first world sports champion. Emily Stowe becomes Canada's first female doctor.
1883		The Sino French War starts: France and China fight over Vietnam. In the end, Vietnam is divided. China controls the north, France gets the south.
1885	The execution of Louis Riel pulls Wilfrid into the political forefront.	The Canadian Pacific Railway is completed. Canada's first national park is created in Banff, Alberta. The Northwest Rebellion takes place. Riel is hanged for treason. The federal government imposes a head tax of $50 on Chinese immigrants.
1887	Wilfrid becomes leader of the federal Liberal party and leader of the Opposition.	
1888		The Fisheries Treaty is passed. The first election takes place in the Northwest Territories.
1891		Sir John A. Macdonald dies while in office. John Abbott becomes the third prime minister of Canada.
1892		Sir John Sparrow David Thompson becomes the fourth prime minister of Canada. The Canadian Criminal Code is established.
1893		An international tribunal decides that Canadians have the right to hunt seals in the Bering Sea. The Stanley Cup is awarded for the first time to the Montreal Amateur Athletic Association hockey club, champions of the Amateur Hockey Association of Canada.
1894		Sir Mackenzie Bowell becomes the fifth prime minister of Canada.
1896	Wilfrid becomes the seventh prime minister. He works out a settlement for the Manitoba schools.	Sir Charles Tupper becomes the sixth prime minister of Canada.
1897	Wilfrid is knighted by Queen Victoria.	The Klondike gold rush occurs. Clara Brett Martin becomes the first woman admitted to the bar of Ontario. Queen Victoria celebrates her diamond (60th) jubilee.
1898		The Yukon Territory is formed. Spanish-American War takes place: Spain loses control over Cuba, Puerto Rico, the Philippine islands, Guam, and other islands.

Even more on the life and times of Sir Wilfrid Laurier

YEAR	WILFRID'S LIFE	EVENTS IN CANADA AND THE WORLD
1899		The first Canadian troops are sent to the South African War. The South African War (Boer War) begins (1899-1902): The British win control of what is now the Republic of South Africa.
1900	Wilfrid sets up the Department of Labour.	The head tax on Chinese immigrants is raised to $100. Boxer Rebellion of China erupts. The Commonwealth of Australia is formed.
1901		Queen Victoria dies.
1903	Wilfrid approves the construction of the second transcontinental railway in Canada.	The Chinese head tax is raised to $500—the equivalent of two years of labour.
1904		The Russo-Japanese War begins: Russia recognizes Japan as the dominant power in Korea and turns over some leased land in the Asian Pacific to Japan. The Trans-Siberian Railway is completed.
1905		Alberta and Saskatchewan become provinces. The Russian revolution occurs: Russians protest against the government of Tsar Nicholas II.
1909	Wilfrid creates the Department of External Affairs.	
1910	Wilfrid creates a Canadian navy.	
1911	The Liberals are defeated in the election. Wilfrid serves as Opposition leader.	Sir Robert Borden becomes Canada's eighth prime minister.
1914		Canada declares war on Germany in September. The War Measures Act is passed. World War I begins on August 1.
1915		The first major battle is fought by Canadians during the First World War. Known as the Battle of Ypres, in Belgium, it lasted from April 22 to May 25.
1916		Manitoba amends its Election Act to allow women to vote in provincial elections.
1917		The conscription crisis occurs. Canadians fight in Battle of Vimy Ridge in France. A "temporary" income tax is introduced. The National Hockey League (NHL) is formed. The Russian revolution ends with the Bolsheviks seizing power.
1918		White women are allowed to vote and are eligible to be candidates in all provinces except Prince Edward Island and Quebec. World War I ends on Armistice Day, November 11. A worldwide influenza epidemic breaks out and kills an estimated 25 million people between 1918 and 1919.
1919	Wilfrid dies on February 17 in Ottawa. He is buried in Notre Dame Cemetery, Ottawa.	Winnipeg General Strike occurs from May 15 to June 26. Canada joins the League of Nations. The Treaty of Versailles is signed on June 28. World War I is over. The League of Nations is established.

Glossary: words and facts you might want to know

Acadians: French people who lived in the French colony of Acadia. Acadia included what is now Nova Scotia, Prince Edward Island, and parts of New Brunswick and Quebec. Acadians began to arrive from France in the early 1600s to take part in the very profitable fur trade. In 1713, France lost control of Acadia to Great Britain. The British wanted to make sure that the Acadians would be loyal to them and demanded that they take an oath of allegiance. The Acadians refused and so, in 1755, the British removed them from their homes and land. They were shipped down to the Thirteen Colonies (now the east coast of the United States) and Louisiana. It is estimated that 11,000 Acadians were deported between 1755 and 1762, when the deportations stopped.

Blake, Edward (1833–1912): Liberal party politician in both the Ontario and federal governments. He was the second premier of Ontario before he joined the federal government under Alexander Mackenzie. He succeeded Mackenzie as Liberal party leader in 1880 but lost the elections of 1882 and 1887. He then resigned his leadership and eventually left Canadian politics in 1891. This made him the only leader of the Liberal Party of Canada not to become prime minister. Although he was born in Upper Canada, he became a member of Parliament in the British House of Commons as an Irish Nationalist from 1892 to 1906. Before entering politics, Edward was a successful and wealthy lawyer. He was recruited into politics by George Brown, owner of the *Toronto Globe* newspaper.

Borden, Sir Robert (1854–1937): defeated Sir Wilfrid Laurier and the Liberals to become Canada's eighth prime minister (1911–1920). He was born in Nova Scotia and worked as a teacher before becoming a lawyer. He entered politics in 1896 as a member of the Conservative party.

British Empire: an old term that refers to Great Britain, all of its dependent countries and provinces, and the British dominions in the world.

Canadian Charter of Rights and Freedoms: part of the Canadian Constitution (the highest laws in the country) that came into effect in 1982. It is meant to protect the rights of minorities and individual citizens. The Canadian charter covers several fields: fundamental rights, democratic rights, mobility rights, legal rights, equality rights, and language rights. All laws in the country that do not agree with the charter have no power.

Canadian Pacific Railway: the first railway to cross Canada from coast to coast. Construction began in 1882. The tracks ran from Montreal to the Pacific coast by the end of 1885. In 1889, the railway became truly transcontinental after tracks were laid through Maine to Saint John, NB.

colonies: groups of people living in a new territory who are governed by the laws of a mother country. For example, Upper and Lower Canada were colonies of England.

Confederation: the union of a group of states or provinces to form a country.

Conservative Party of Canada: the first party to govern the Dominion of Canada. It began in 1854 when politicians from Upper and Lower Canada joined to form a coalition government of the Province of Canada. It was initially called the Liberal-Conservative party but changed its name to the Conservative party when a separate Liberal party was formed at the time of Confederation. Sir John A. Macdonald was its first leader.

Éthier, Adéline: second wife of Carolus Laurier and stepmother of Sir Wilfrid. Adéline had always been part of the Laurier household in her role as maid. She helped nurse first Marcelle and then Malvina through their final months of life. With Carolus, she had four sons and two daughters. One of her sons, Ubald, Wilfrid's half-brother, was an elected member of Parliament in the Liberal party from 1900 until his death in 1906.

honourary degree: an academic degree awarded to an individual for their outstanding life achievements rather than for their university studies. An honourary degree may be granted by a university that the recipient never attended. Usually the degree is presented with great ceremony as a way of honouring a famous or distinguished visitor.

House of Commons: the lower house of Parliament. It consists of a Speaker, the prime minister and his cabinet, members of the governing party, members of the opposition parties, and sometimes a few independent members (elected members who do not belong to an official party).

More words and facts you might want to know

The members of the House (called members of Parliament or MPs) are elected in constituency elections or by-elections by the Canadian people. The House (often incorrectly referred to as Parliament) is important because it is where all new laws start.

Hudson's Bay Company: the business that was incorporated in England in 1670 to trade fur with the First Nations people and control all lands whose rivers and streams drained into Hudson Bay. This huge area, called Rupert's Land, stretched from Labrador, across modern-day Quebec and Ontario, to south of the present United States/Canada border and west to the Canadian Rocky Mountains. In 1870, the HBC sold most of Rupert's Land to the Canadian government. The company evolved into the chain of retail stores now known as "The Bay."

King James Bible: the English translation of the Bible that is used by English-speaking Protestants. In 1604, King James I of England appointed 54 scholars to translate it from Latin, which had been the official language of the Church. After seven years, the King James version was completed. There had been earlier attempts at translating the Bible into English (from as early as 1382) but there were errors and the language was hard to understand. As the English language continued to change, a revised version was written in the later 1800s to clear up words that people no longer understood.

Klondike: region of the Yukon Territory, just east of the Alaska border. It lies around the Klondike River, which is a stream that feeds into the Yukon River. In 1896, rich deposits of gold were discovered in the gravel of a creek that fed into the Klondike River. Put a couple of shovels full of dirt in a pan, swirl it around in the water and voila, you've got gold! The Klondike gold rush was on. News of the discovery reached the United States in July 1897, and within a month thousands of people were rushing north. Over 25,000 people were in the Klondike by 1898. By the summer of 1899, the stampede was over because mining by hand had become too hard. News of another gold strike in Alaska lured most of the people away from the Klondike.

Knight of the British Empire: the honour given to someone by the king or queen of Great Britain as a reward for personal excellence or services provided to the crown or country. This is how people come to use the title "Sir" in their name.

Lafontaine, Zoé (1841–1921): wife of Sir Wilfrid. They met while both boarded with Dr. Séraphin Gauthier in Montreal. They married in 1868 and did not have children. She died in Ottawa on November 1, 1921, almost three years after her husband.

Laurier, Carolus: father of Sir Wilfrid. He was a bilingual farmer and surveyor who loved to read and meet people. Carolus was a natural leader who became the first mayor of St-Lin in 1855. He and his father were interested in politics, especially the policies of Louis-Joseph Papineau's Parti patriote. With his first wife Marcelle Martineau, he had three children. After Marcelle died, he married Adéline Éthier, with whom he had six more children.

Laurier, Malvina (1844–1856): sister of Sir Wilfrid. She died of tuberculosis, just like her mother, when she was 11 years old.

Lavergne, Armand Renaud (1880-1935): lawyer, politician, and son of Émilie Barthe, who was the wife of Wilfrid's law partner Joseph Lavergne. Armand's physical resemblance to Wilfrid made people wonder if he was Wilfrid's son. He was a member of Parliament in Ottawa and the Legislative Assembly of Quebec at different times in his political career. He switched parties over the years: Liberal, Nationalist, and finally Conservative. He was ahead of his time when he proposed in 1907 that English and French be treated equally in public matters. It took until 1969 to be enacted. He died while in office as deputy speaker of the House of Commons in R. B. Bennett's government.

Liberal Party of Canada: the second party to govern the Dominion of Canada. The party was formed in 1867, after Canada's Confederation. Canada's second prime minister was a Liberal, Sir Alexander Mackenzie.

Lower Canada (1791–1840): province created by the Constitutional Act of 1791, which divided the former Province of Quebec into two parts: Upper Canada and Lower Canada. These two provinces were joined once again to form the Province of Canada in 1841 and were also known as Canada West (Upper Canada or Ontario) and Canada East (Lower Canada or Quebec).

More words and facts you might want to know

Macdonald, Sir John A.
(1815–1891): Canada's first prime minister (1867–1873, 1878–1891). Born in Scotland, he moved to Upper Canada with his family in 1820. He trained and worked as a lawyer before becoming involved in politics. He spent many years working on bringing the Province of Canada and the Maritime provinces together. On July 1, 1867, his dream came true with the creation of the Dominion of Canada. He died while in office in Ottawa.

Mackenzie, Alexander (1822–92): second prime minister of Canada (1873–78) who formed the first Liberal government in the Dominion of Canada. Born in Scotland, he immigrated to Canada in 1842. He worked as a stone mason, a building contractor, and a newspaper editor before entering politics.

Martineau, Marcelle (1815–1848): mother of Sir Wilfrid and first wife of Carolus. She and Carolus had three children: Honorine, who died when she was only three; Sir Wilfrid; and Malvina. Marcelle was a gentle person who loved books and music and enjoyed painting. She died of tuberculosis when Wilfrid was seven years old.

member of Parliament: politician who is elected to sit in the House of Commons. During a general election, the country is divided up into ridings (or "constituencies"). The voters in each riding elect one candidate to represent them as their member of Parliament.

Métis: a person whose ancestry is half First Nations and half French Canadian. Métis culture combines both backgrounds.

Northwest Rebellion (1885): the second rebellion led by Louis Riel. By the 1880s, European and other settlers were moving into modern-day Saskatchewan; the Métis saw their traditional lifestyle threatened. First Nations people had signed treaties giving up claim to the whole of the territory and agreed to settle on reserves. The Canadian government, however, did not live up to its end of the deal. The Métis of Saskatchewan invited Louis Riel to help them. He set up a provisional government, which was eventually overthrown by Canadian troops. Riel surrendered and was hanged for treason.

Papineau, Louis-Joseph
(1786–1871): a wealthy *seigneur* (land owner) in Lower Canada (now Quebec). He was a strong supporter of the Roman Catholic Church and the traditional *Canadien* (French) way of life. While a member of the Legislative Assembly of Lower Canada, he became leader of the Parti patriote and promoted the American style of government. He felt that even though French Canadians made up the majority of the population they had less control in the government than the English. He supported the Rebellion of 1837 but fled to the United States before it was over. He was granted amnesty (pardoned) in 1844 and returned home in 1845. He re-entered politics and influenced a new group of young politicians who later became the Parti rouge.

Parti bleu: the political group formed in about 1850 in Canada East (formerly Lower Canada, now Quebec) by believers of moderate reform in the colony. Members believed that they should co-operate with British colonists to ensure

that their language and culture survived. They believed that confederating with English-speaking colonies would result in the old Province of Quebec being re-established. The name *bleu* was chosen to distinguish the party from the extremist, anti-church Parti rouge. The Parti bleu (with members sometimes known as les bleus) was very popular and had the support of Roman Catholic Church leaders. The party allied itself with the Liberal-Conservative party in Canada West and together they formed the basis for the future Conservative Party of Canada.

Parti rouge: the political party formed in 1848 in Canada East (formerly Lower Canada, now Quebec) by young intellectual francophones who were followers of Louis-Joseph Papineau's ideas. Members of the party, called *les rouges*, wanted to undo the Act of the Union, 1841, which united Upper and Lower Canada into a single colony, the Province of Canada. Also, les rouges wanted to have Canada East annexed to the United States. The party also insisted that the Church and the state should be separate. After Confederation, the Parti rouge merged with the Reform party to form the Liberal party.

Patriotes: named in 1826, the political party in Lower Canada (now Quebec) that called for reforms to make the government more fair and democratic for the majority French-speaking inhabitants, who opposed being in a British colony. Under the leadership of Louis-Joseph Papineau, members wanted to preserve the *Canadien* (French) way of life, values, and institutions. In 1834, the

Still more words and facts you might want to know

Patriotes presented their complaints to the British government in a document called the "Ninety-Two Resolutions." Great Britain rejected their calls for reform, which led to the Rebellions of 1837–38. Following the failed rebellion, the party disappeared.

Plains of Abraham: site of a battle between French and British armies on September 13, 1759. It lies three kilometres from Quebec City, the centre of French power in North America. The battle was over in less than an hour—the British took Quebec City. The struggle for the rest of French North America continued until the French surrendered to the British in 1760.

Quebec Assembly: now known as the Assemblée nationale, it is the provincial body that represents the people of Quebec. Situated in Quebec City, it is composed of one member from each of the province's ridings and is headed by the *premier ministre* (premier) and his cabinet ministers.

Queen Victoria (1819–1901): Queen of the United Kingdom of Great Britain and Ireland (1837–1901) and empress of India (1876–1901). She gave her name to an era, the Victorian Age.

Rebellion of 1837: failed uprising of Canadiens (French-speaking people) in Lower Canada against the British in November and December, 1837. The majority of people in Lower Canada were francophone but the colony was governed by the British. Under the leadership of Louis-Joseph Papineau and his party Les Patriotes, members of the Lower Canada Assembly (government) demanded more power for the people. In the name of democracy, they wanted to control how the money for the colony was spent and slow the influx of English-speaking people. Great Britain rejected their demands, which led to demonstrations and finally an armed rebellion. Papineau and other leaders fled to the United States. A rebellion also took place in Upper Canada, led by William Lyon Mackenzie, who tried to take advantage of British troops leaving for the rebellion in Lower Canada.

Red River Rebellion (1869–70): the events in which the Métis of Red River (modern-day Manitoba) took up arms against the Canadian government. The crisis arose when the Hudson's Bay Company agreed to sell Rupert's Land, which included Red River, to Canada. In protest, Louis Riel and other Métis proclaimed a provisional government to negotiate with Canada. Things turned violent when some Canadian settlers took up arms against the Métis. The Canadian government responded by sending troops to enforce federal authority. Riel fled before the expedition arrived and went into exile in the United States. The Canadian government eventually agreed to meet some of the demands of the Métis. The result was the Manitoba Act, which created the province of Manitoba.

Reform party: political party in Canada West (now Ontario) that led the opposition to the ruling Conservatives and campaigned for responsible government (more control for the elected members of the government). Led by George Brown, the party formed a short-lived government in the Province of Canada with the Parti rouge of Canada East (now Quebec) in 1858. In 1867, the Reform and Rouge parties merged to form the Liberal party.

Riel, Louis (1844–1885): a Métis lawyer who led two armed rebellions against the Canadian government to defend the rights and lands of the French and First Nations people in the territories that later became Manitoba and Saskatchewan. Riel led the Red River Rebellion in 1869, then went into exile in the United States, fearing for his safety. He later moved to Saskatchewan, where he led the Northwest Rebellion in 1885. This rebellion was quickly crushed and Riel was hanged for treason.

Sifton, Sir Clifford (1861–1929): lawyer, politician, and newspaper owner. His work was important in making the Canadian West a vital agricultural area. As Canada's minister of the interior from 1896 to 1905, Sifton persuaded the government to increase immigration in order to increase farm production in the West. To attract as many newcomers as possible, Sifton established Canadian offices throughout Britain, in some European countries, and in the United States. He resigned in 1905 because he disagreed with his government's involvement in creating separate Catholic schools in the newly formed provinces of Alberta and Saskatchewan. He owned the *Manitoba Free Press* between 1891 and 1921. He was knighted in 1915.

Index